Jo Petty's

Words
to *Live By*

Jo Petty's

Words to Live By

A Treasury of Favorite Sayings

INSPIRATIONAL PRESS

New York

Portions of this work have appeared previously in: *Apples of Gold* copyright © 1962 by Jo Petty; *Treasures of Silver* copyright © 1977 by The C.R. Gibson Company, Norwalk, Connecticut; *Wings of Silver* copyright © 1967 by The C.R. Gibson Company, Norwalk, Connecticut; *Promises and Premises* copyright © 1972 by The C.R. Gibson Company.

First Inspirational Press edition published in 1995.

INSPIRATIONAL PRESS
A division of Budget Book Service, Inc.
386 Park Avenue South, New York, NY 10016

Inspirational Press is a registered trademark of Budget Book Service, Inc.
Published by arrangement with The C.R. Gibson Company.
Library of Congress Catalog Card Number: 95-79146   ISBN: 0-88486-123-6

Printed in the United States of America

Foreword

*C*ulled from many different sources, these eloquent and heartfelt praises celebrate the basic Christian virtures—love, faith, goodness, meekness, joy, suffering, gentleness, temperance, peace—that have served as a cornerstone for all my devotional works.

These writings have been a constant source of inspiration and spiritual sustenance to me in my daily life, and I share them with you, my beloved readers, in the hope that they will set your hearts singing and spirits soaring.

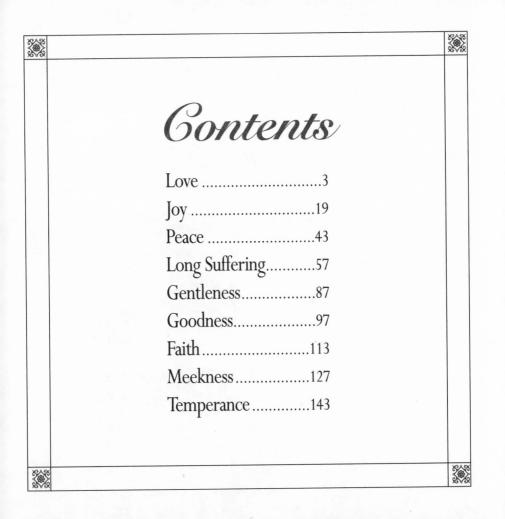

Contents

Real friends are those who,
when you've made a fool of yourself,
don't feel that you've done a permanent job.

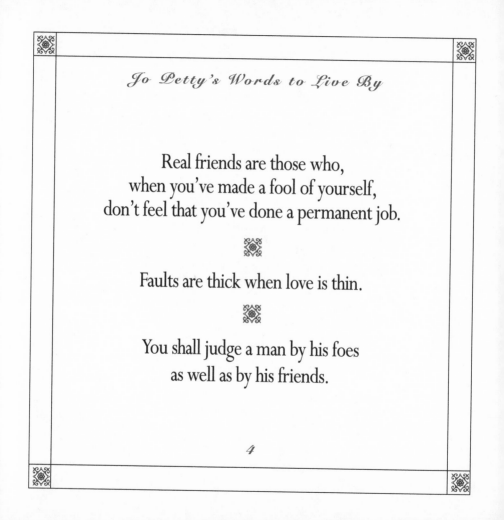

Faults are thick when love is thin.

You shall judge a man by his foes
as well as by his friends.

Friendship is to be purchased
only by friendship.

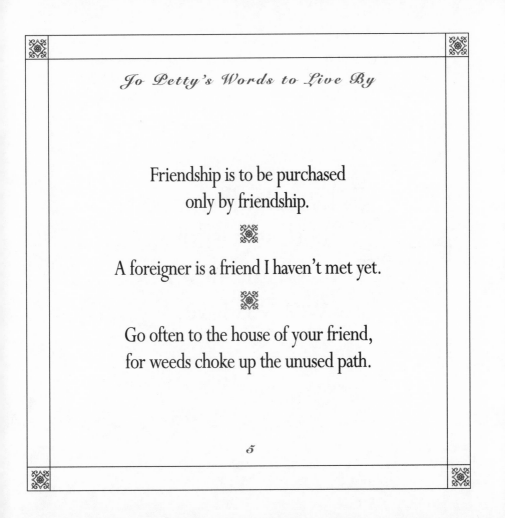

A foreigner is a friend I haven't met yet.

Go often to the house of your friend,
for weeds choke up the unused path.

To learn and never be
filled, is wisdom;
To teach and never be
weary is love.

Love praises others.

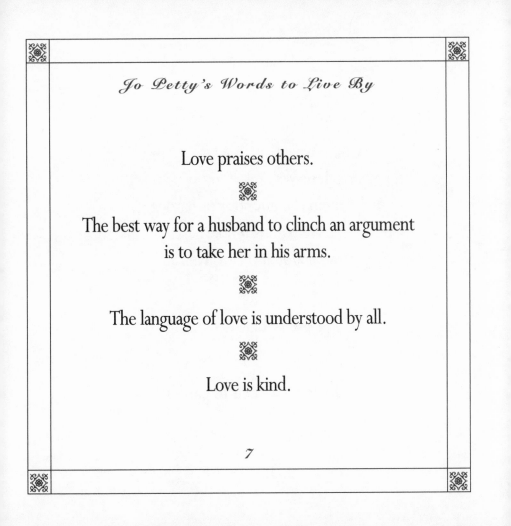

The best way for a husband to clinch an argument
is to take her in his arms.

The language of love is understood by all.

Love is kind.

Come what may, hold fast to love!
Though men should rend your heart,
let them not embitter or harden it.
We win by tenderness;
we conquer by forgiveness.

Love is the law of life.

To understand is to pardon.

The smallest
good deed
is better than
the grandest
intention.

The best gifts are tied with heartstrings.

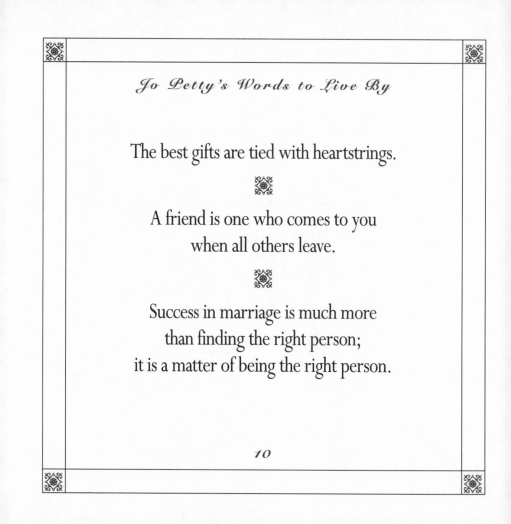

A friend is one who comes to you
when all others leave.

Success in marriage is much more
than finding the right person;
it is a matter of being the right person.

Let us love
in deed and in truth
rather than in
word and tongue.

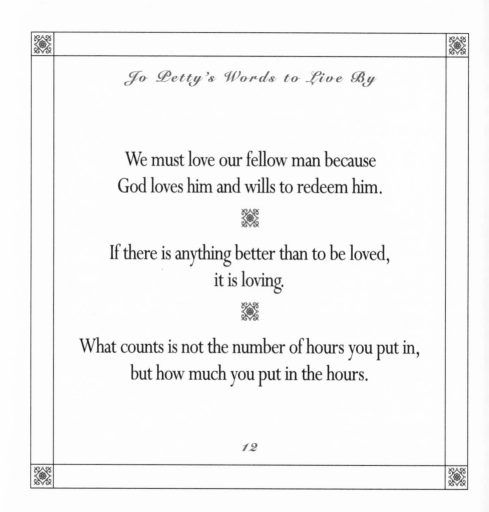

We must love our fellow man because
God loves him and wills to redeem him.

If there is anything better than to be loved,
it is loving.

What counts is not the number of hours you put in,
but how much you put in the hours.

The heart
has reasons
that reason
does not
understand.

Teach me, Father, when I pray,
Not to ask for more,
But rather let me give thanks
For what is at my door.
For food and drink, for gentle rain,
For sunny skies above,
For home and friends, for peace and joy,
But most of all for LOVE.

The coin of God's realm is love.

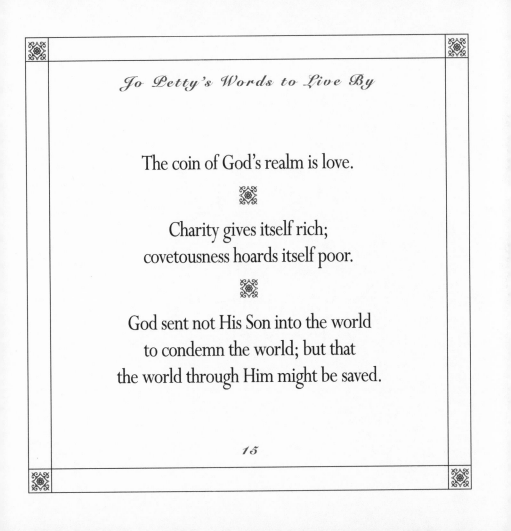

Charity gives itself rich;
covetousness hoards itself poor.

God sent not His Son into the world
to condemn the world; but that
the world through Him might be saved.

God pardons
like a mother,
who kisses the offense
into everlasting
forgetfulness.

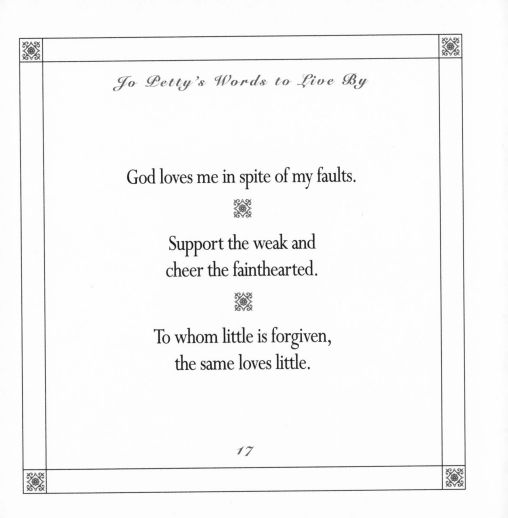

God loves me in spite of my faults.

Support the weak and
cheer the fainthearted.

To whom little is forgiven,
the same loves little.

Joy

Do you see difficulties in every opportunity
or opportunities in every difficulty?

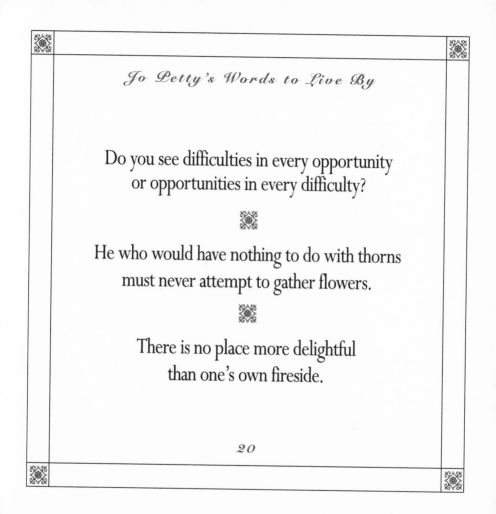

He who would have nothing to do with thorns
must never attempt to gather flowers.

There is no place more delightful
than one's own fireside.

Yes, it's pretty hard, the optimistic
old woman admitted. I have to get along
with only two teeth—one upper, one lower—
but, thank goodness, they meet.

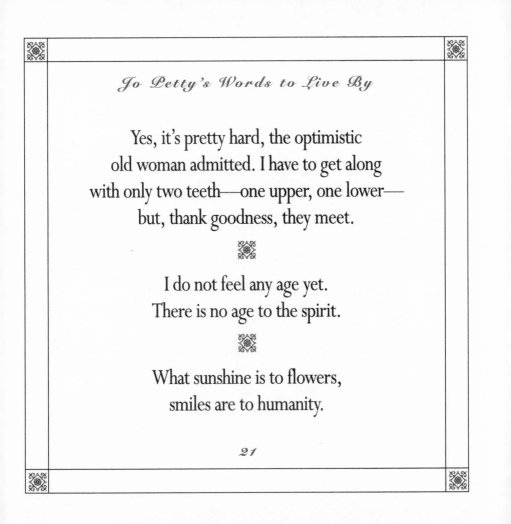

I do not feel any age yet.
There is no age to the spirit.

What sunshine is to flowers,
smiles are to humanity.

I want a soul so full of joy—
Life's withering storms cannot destroy.

So long as enthusiasm lasts,
so long is youth still with us.

It is good to let a little sunshine
out as well as in.

Growing old
is no more
than a bad habit
which a busy person
has no time to form.

It takes both rain and sunshine
to make a rainbow.

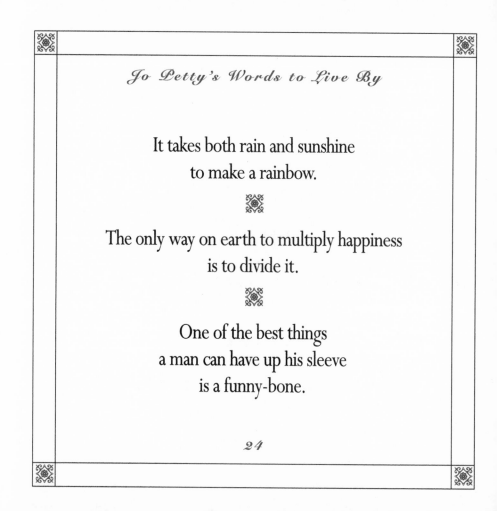

The only way on earth to multiply happiness
is to divide it.

One of the best things
a man can have up his sleeve
is a funny-bone.

People are lonely because they build walls instead of bridges.

The secret of being miserable
is to have the leisure
to bother about whether you are happy or not.

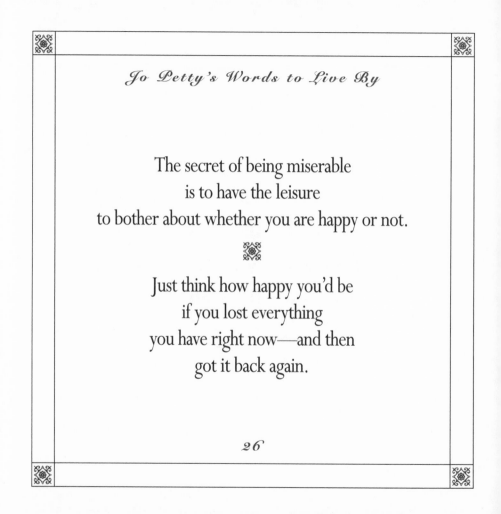

Just think how happy you'd be
if you lost everything
you have right now—and then
got it back again.

When a man has a "pet peeve"
it's remarkable how often he pets it.

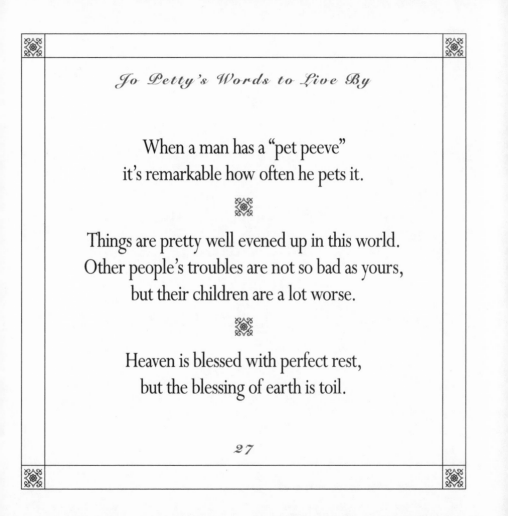

Things are pretty well evened up in this world.
Other people's troubles are not so bad as yours,
but their children are a lot worse.

Heaven is blessed with perfect rest,
but the blessing of earth is toil.

27

Better to light
one candle
than to curse
the darkness.

Humdrum is not where you live;
it's what you are.

If we learn how to give ourselves, to forgive others,
and to live with thanksgiving
we need not seek happiness—it will seek us.

A humorist is a man who feels bad
but feels good about it.

29

That load becomes light
which is cheerfully borne.

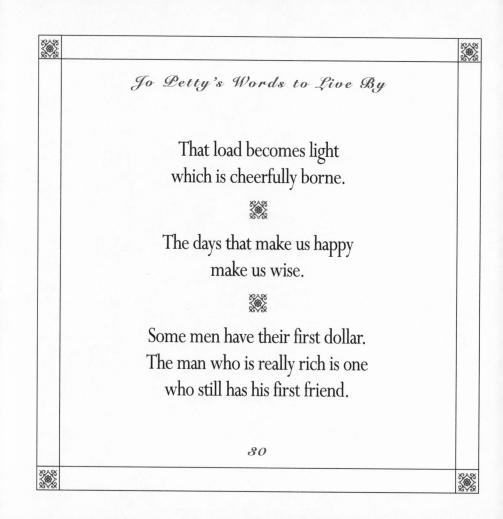

The days that make us happy
make us wise.

Some men have their first dollar.
The man who is really rich is one
who still has his first friend.

30

He who has not forgiven
an enemy has never yet tasted
one of the most sublime
enjoyments of life.

To speak kindly does not hurt the tongue.

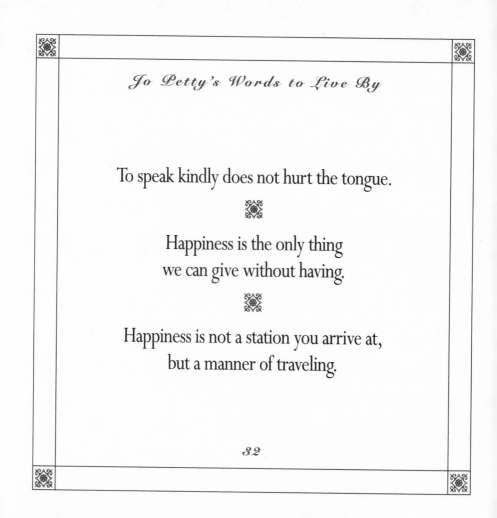

Happiness is the only thing
we can give without having.

Happiness is not a station you arrive at,
but a manner of traveling.

All the flowers of all the tomorrows
are in the seeds of today.

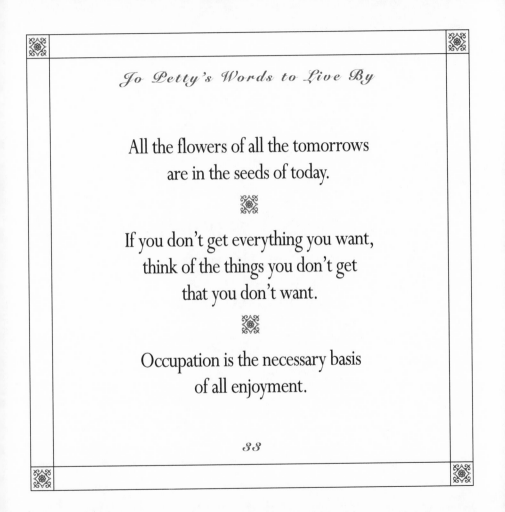

If you don't get everything you want,
think of the things you don't get
that you don't want.

Occupation is the necessary basis
of all enjoyment.

He enjoys much
who is thankful
for little.

Happiness is not a reward—
it is a consequence.

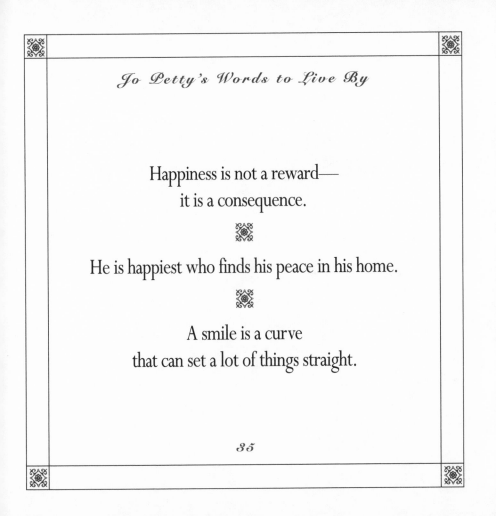

He is happiest who finds his peace in his home.

A smile is a curve
that can set a lot of things straight.

Few pleasures are more lasting
than reading a good book.

Sorrow, like rain, makes roses and mud.

Each new day is a chance
to start all over again.

The foolish man
seeks happiness
in the distance;
the wise man
grows it under his feet.

I may be rich and have nothing.

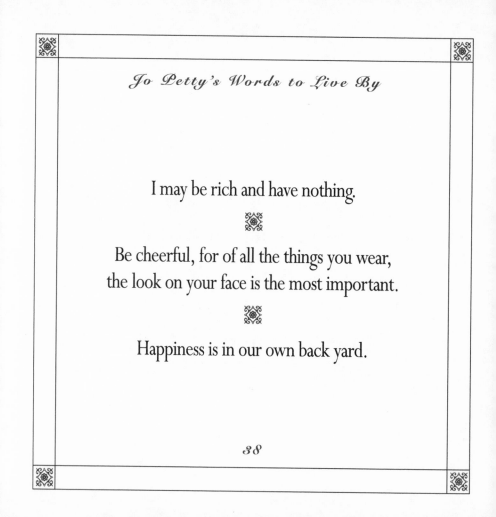

Be cheerful, for of all the things you wear,
the look on your face is the most important.

Happiness is in our own back yard.

Be the labor
great or small—
Do it well
or not at all.

We cannot have mountains without valleys.

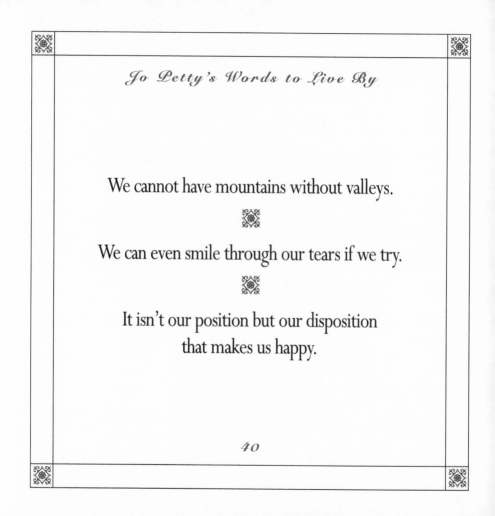

We can even smile through our tears if we try.

It isn't our position but our disposition
that makes us happy.

Happiness is a thing to be practiced
like a violin.

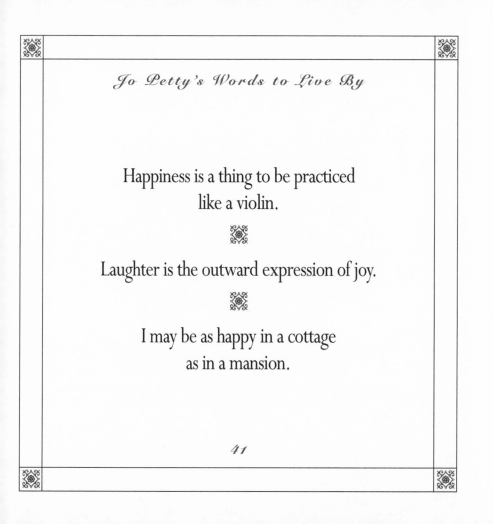

Laughter is the outward expression of joy.

I may be as happy in a cottage
as in a mansion.

One who is afraid
of lying
is usually afraid
of nothing else.

Worry never climbed a hill
Worry never paid a bill
Worry never dried a tear
Worry never calmed a fear
Worry never darned a heel
Worry never cooked a meal
Worry never led a horse to water
Worry never done a thing
you'd think it oughta.

The light that shows us our sin
is the light that heals us.

To be a seeker is soon to be a finder.

With God all things are possible.

If God be for me,
who can be against me?

The secret of contentment
is know how to enjoy what you have.

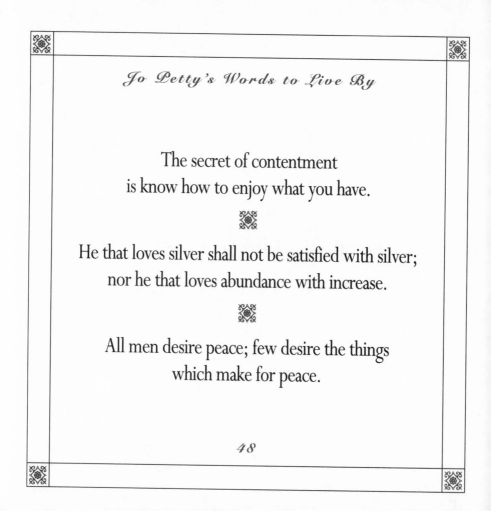

He that loves silver shall not be satisfied with silver;
nor he that loves abundance with increase.

All men desire peace; few desire the things
which make for peace.

Well-arranged time is the surest mark
of a well-arranged mind.

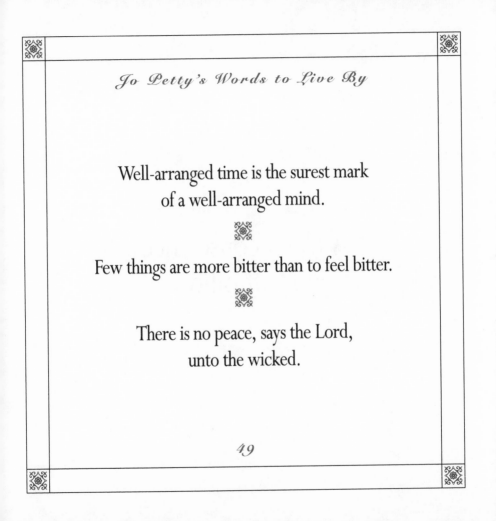

Few things are more bitter than to feel bitter.

There is no peace, says the Lord,
unto the wicked.

A clean conscience
is a soft pillow.

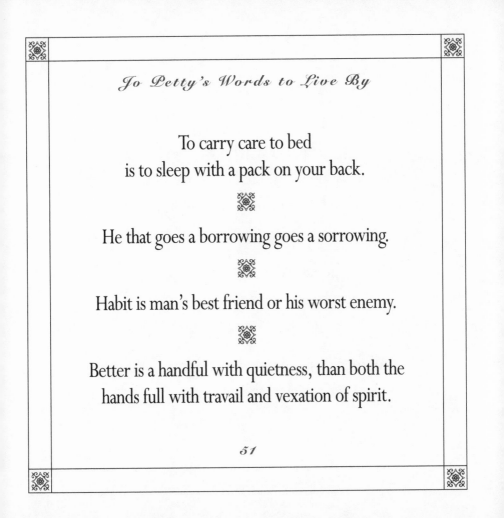

To carry care to bed
is to sleep with a pack on your back.

He that goes a borrowing goes a sorrowing.

Habit is man's best friend or his worst enemy.

Better is a handful with quietness, than both the
hands full with travail and vexation of spirit.

The fellow who worries
about what people think of him wouldn't worry
so much if he only knew how seldom they do.

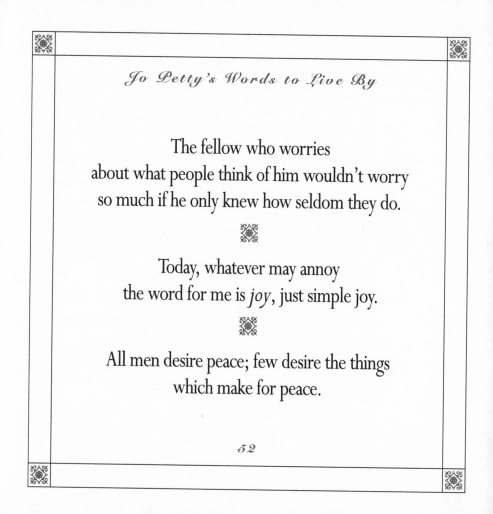

Today, whatever may annoy
the word for me is *joy*, just simple joy.

All men desire peace; few desire the things
which make for peace.

Peace is not
the absence of conflict,
but the ability
to cope with it.

We cannot always control what happens around us,
but we can control how we feel about it.

Don't hurry, don't worry,
Do your best, and leave the rest.

Life is like licking honey off a thorn.

A minute of thought
is worth more
than an hour of talk.

*Long
Suffering*

People who
fly into a rage
always make
a bad landing.

There is no failure save in giving up.

❈

A mistake at least proves somebody stopped talking
long enough to do something.

❈

The diamond cannot be polished without friction,
nor man perfected without trials.

The secret of patience
is doing something else in the meanwhile.

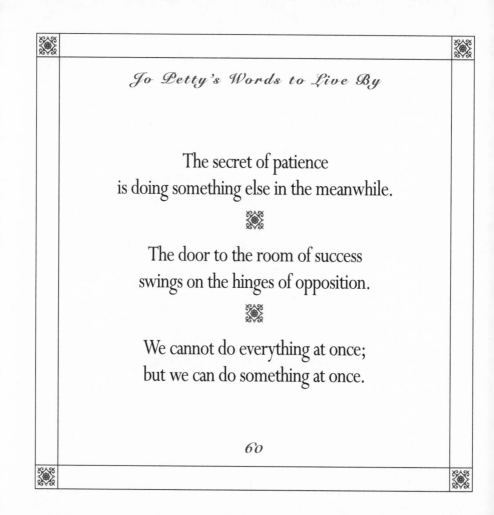

The door to the room of success
swings on the hinges of opposition.

We cannot do everything at once;
but we can do something at once.

Whoever has resigned
himself to fate,
will find that fate
accepts his resignation.

Itching for what you want
doesn't do much good;
you've got to scratch for it.

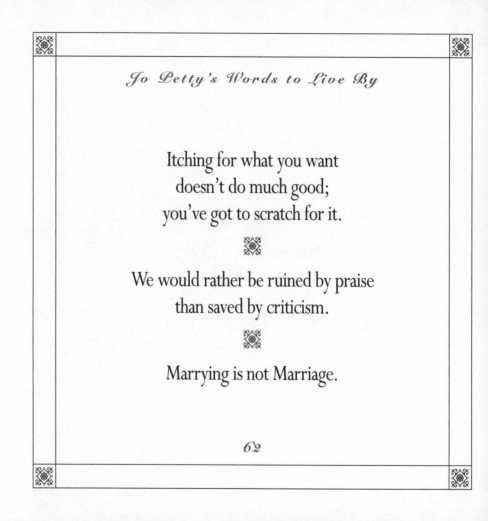

We would rather be ruined by praise
than saved by criticism.

Marrying is not Marriage.

A diamond is a
piece of coal
that stuck to the job.

The Lord sometimes takes us into troubled waters
not to drown us, but to cleanse us.

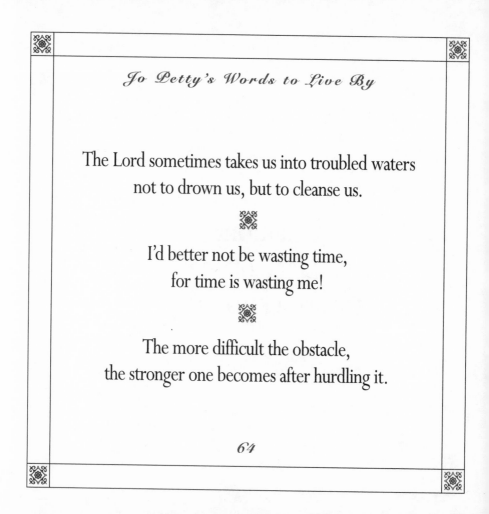

I'd better not be wasting time,
for time is wasting me!

The more difficult the obstacle,
the stronger one becomes after hurdling it.

No difficulties, no discovery,
No pains, no gains.

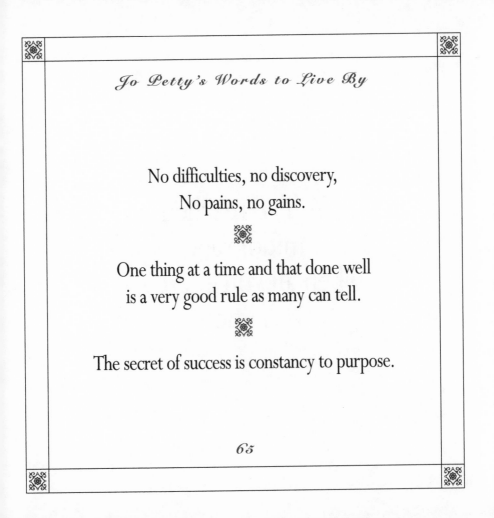

One thing at a time and that done well
is a very good rule as many can tell.

The secret of success is constancy to purpose.

You've reached
middle age
when all you exercise
is caution.

Difficulties strengthen the mind,
as labor does the body.

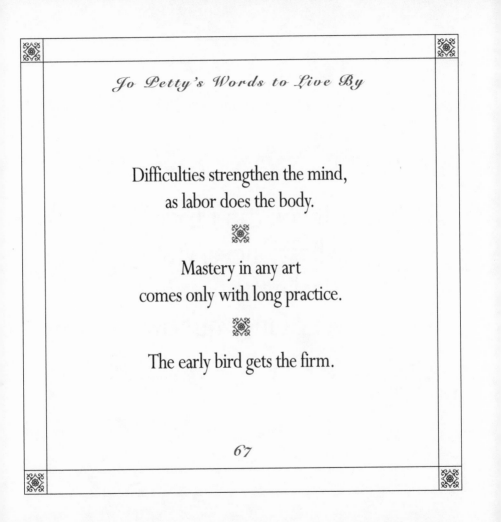

Mastery in any art
comes only with long practice.

The early bird gets the firm.

67

If you can't have
the best of everything,
make the best of
everything you have.

Making excuses doesn't
change the truth.

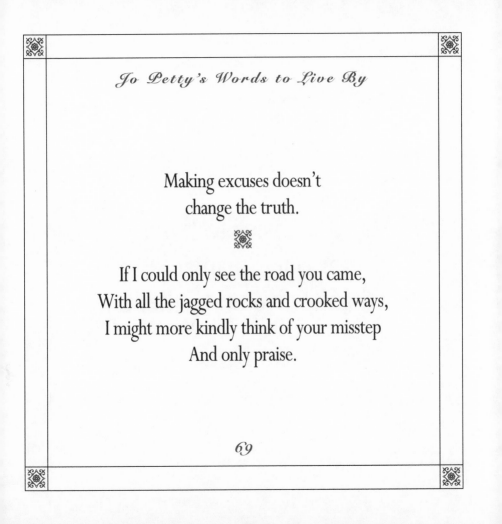

If I could only see the road you came,
With all the jagged rocks and crooked ways,
I might more kindly think of your misstep
And only praise.

It is easier to fight
for one's principles
than to live up to them.

The dictionary is the only place
success comes before work.

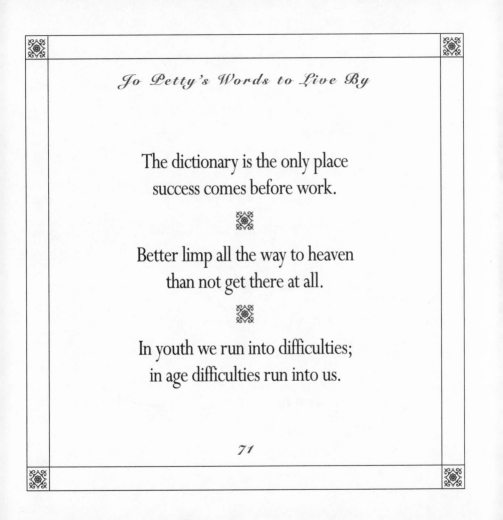

Better limp all the way to heaven
than not get there at all.

In youth we run into difficulties;
in age difficulties run into us.

Patience is not passive; on the contrary it is active;
it is concentrated strength.

You can tell some people aren't afraid of work
by the way they fight it.

All people are born equal.
Each has a right to earn his niche
by the sweat of his brow.
But some sweat more and carve larger niches.

Adversity is
the only balance
to weigh friends–
prosperity is
no just scale.

You can't slide uphill.

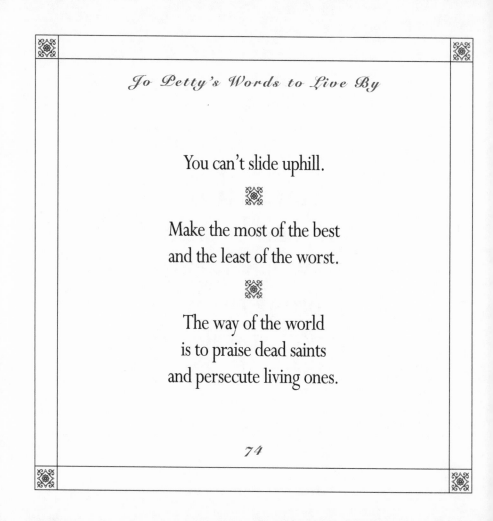

Make the most of the best
and the least of the worst.

The way of the world
is to praise dead saints
and persecute living ones.

It is the practice of the multitudes
to bark at eminent men
as little dogs at strangers.

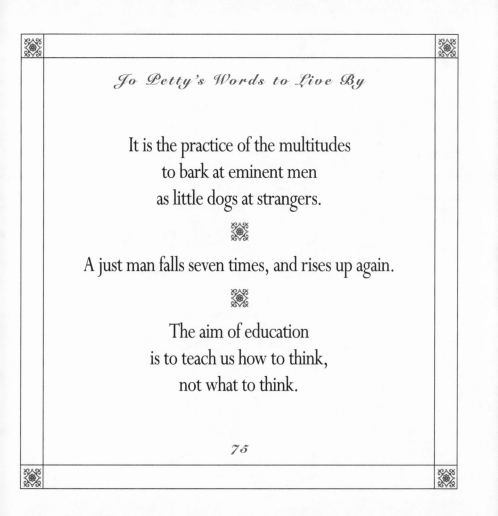

A just man falls seven times, and rises up again.

The aim of education
is to teach us how to think,
not what to think.

It is by those
who have suffered
that the world is most
advanced.

Talent knows what to do;
tact knows when and how to do it.

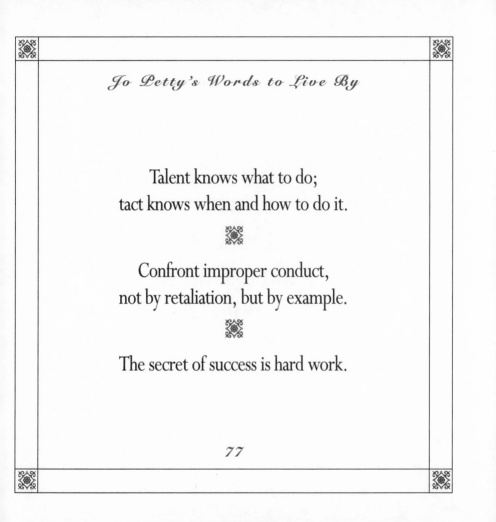

Confront improper conduct,
not by retaliation, but by example.

The secret of success is hard work.

77

An obstinate man
does not
hold opinions—
they hold him.

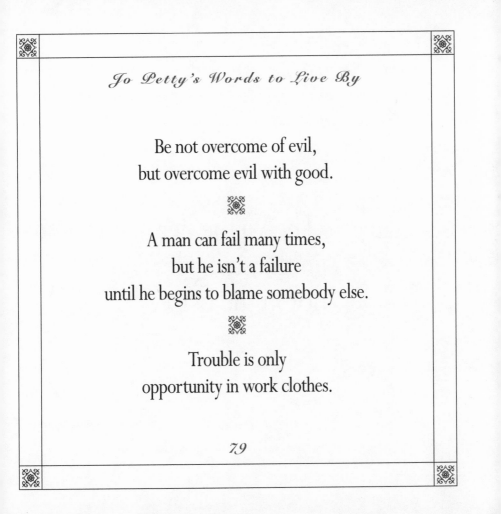

Be not overcome of evil,
but overcome evil with good.

A man can fail many times,
but he isn't a failure
until he begins to blame somebody else.

Trouble is only
opportunity in work clothes.

The virtue lies
in the struggle,
not in the prize.

Failing is not falling,
but in failing to rise when you fall.

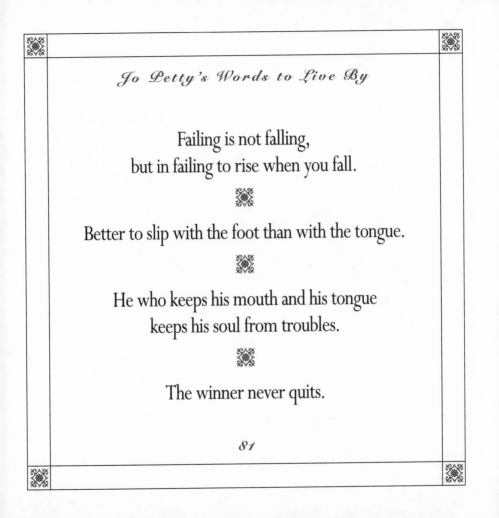

Better to slip with the foot than with the tongue.

He who keeps his mouth and his tongue
keeps his soul from troubles.

The winner never quits.

There's no sense
in advertising your troubles.
There is no market for them.

When music speaks,
all other voices should cease.

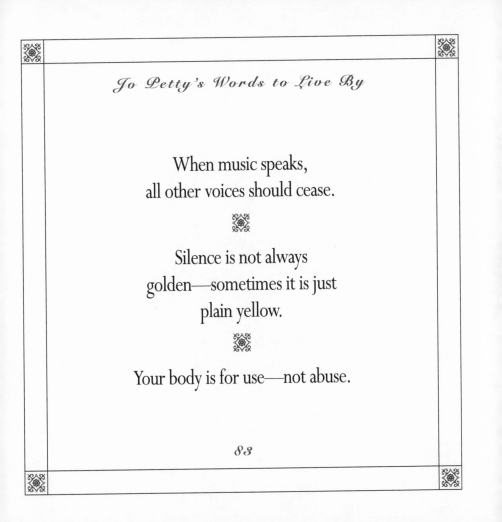

Silence is not always
golden—sometimes it is just
plain yellow.

Your body is for use—not abuse.

Spend less than you get.

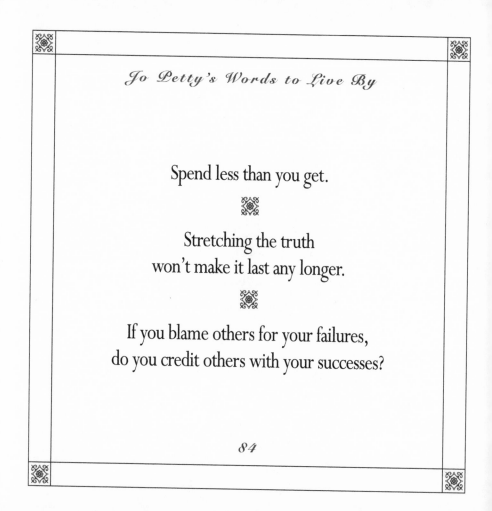

Stretching the truth
won't make it last any longer.

If you blame others for your failures,
do you credit others with your successes?

The greatest
and sublimest power
is often simple patience.

Gentleness

The merciful shall obtain mercy.

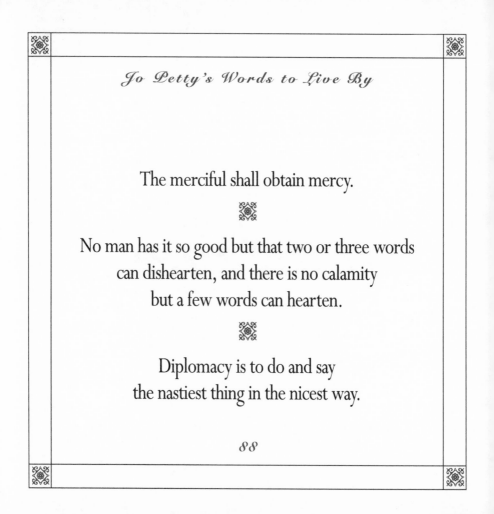

No man has it so good but that two or three words
can dishearten, and there is no calamity
but a few words can hearten.

Diplomacy is to do and say
the nastiest thing in the nicest way.

I have wept in the night
for the shortness of sight
That to somebody's need made me blind;
But I never have yet felt a twinge of regret
For being a little too kind.

The milk of human kindness
never curdles.

He who reforms himself
has done much toward
reforming others.

It is more blessed to give than to receive.

❈

Today's profits are yesterday's goodwill ripened.

❈

Punctuality is the politeness of kings
and the duty of gentle people everywhere.

A soft answer turns away wrath,
but grievous words stir up anger.

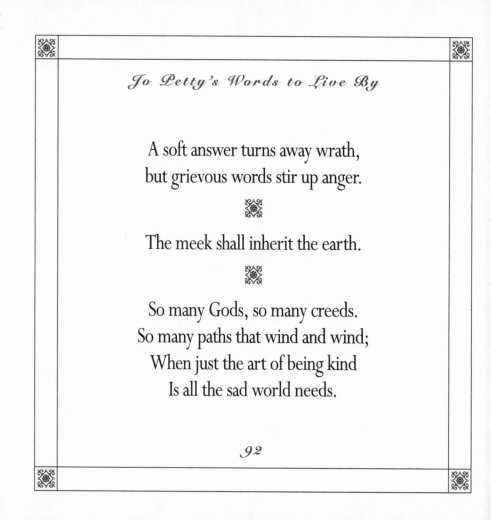

The meek shall inherit the earth.

So many Gods, so many creeds.
So many paths that wind and wind;
When just the art of being kind
Is all the sad world needs.

Nothing is so strong
as gentleness,
nothing so gentle
as real strength.

An admission of error
is a sign of strength rather than
a confession of weakness.

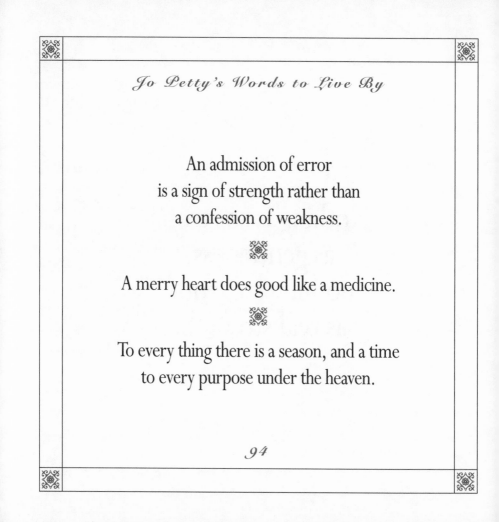

A merry heart does good like a medicine.

To every thing there is a season, and a time
to every purpose under the heaven.

Be what you wish
others to become.

Goodness

The wicked borrows, and pays not again:
but the righteous shows mercy and gives.

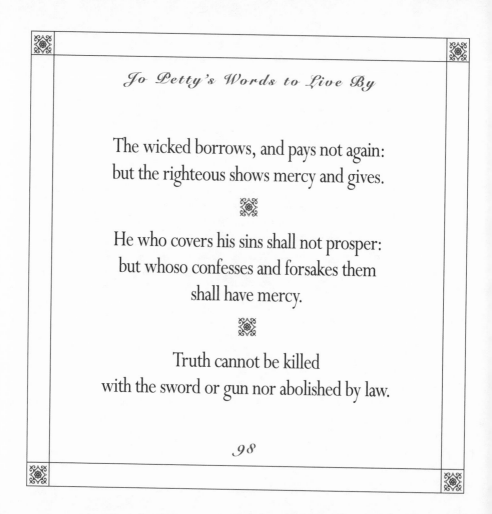

He who covers his sins shall not prosper:
but whoso confesses and forsakes them
shall have mercy.

Truth cannot be killed
with the sword or gun nor abolished by law.

If the whole world followed you,
Followed to the letter,
Tell me—if it followed you,
Would the world be better?

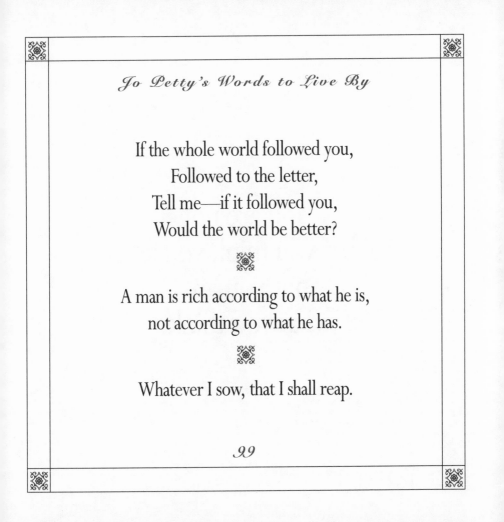

A man is rich according to what he is,
not according to what he has.

Whatever I sow, that I shall reap.

You are not
what you think you are,
but you are
what you think.

You are not better for being praised
nor worse for being blamed.

Honest gain is the only permanent gain.

Pretty is as pretty does.

Oh, what a tangled web we weave,
when first we practice to deceive.

The rung of a ladder was never meant to rest upon,
but only to hold a man's foot long enough
to enable him to put the other one higher.

Whosoever shall smite you on your right cheek,
turn to him the other also.

The hand that's dirty with honest labor
is fit to shake with any neighbor.

Honesty is always the best policy.

It is better to suffer for speaking the truth than that
the truth should suffer for want of speaking it.

The only way
to settle a disagreement
is on the basis of what's
right—not who's right.

The measure of a man's real character
is what he would do if he knew
he would never be found out.

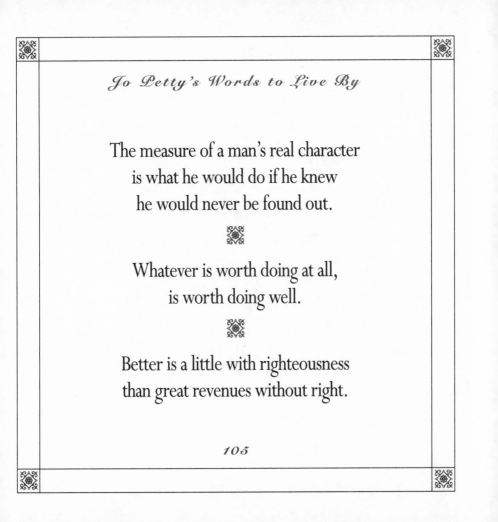

Whatever is worth doing at all,
is worth doing well.

Better is a little with righteousness
than great revenues without right.

There may be times when you cannot find help,
but there is not time when you cannot give help.

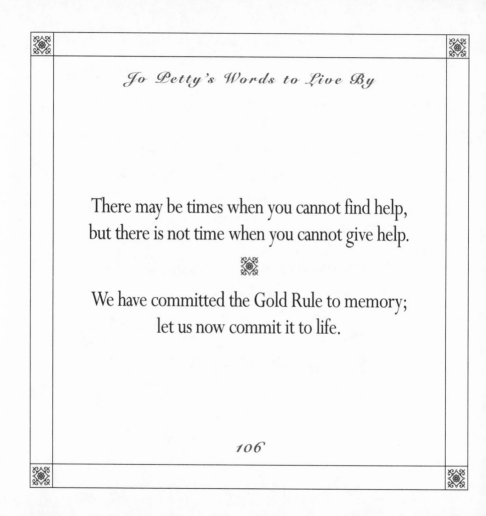

We have committed the Gold Rule to memory;
let us now commit it to life.

There is so much good in the worst of us,
and so much bad in the best of us,
that it behooves all of us
not to talk about the rest of us.

❖

Truth is the foundation of all knowledge
and the cement of all societies.

He who is not liberal
with what he has
deceives himself
when he thinks
he would be liberal
if he had more.

The world is slowly learning that because two men
think differently neither need be wicked.

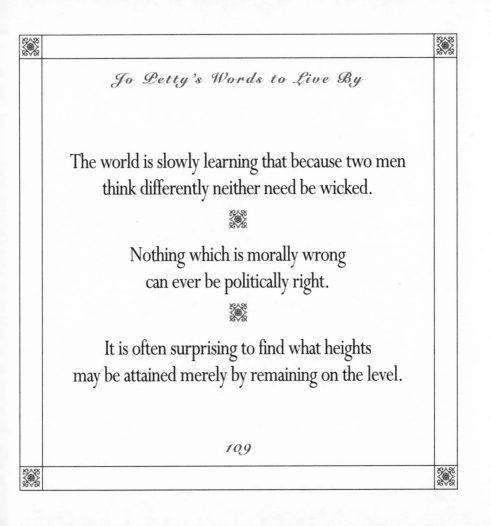

Nothing which is morally wrong
can ever be politically right.

It is often surprising to find what heights
may be attained merely by remaining on the level.

The Devil has many tools,
but a lie is the handle
that fits them all.

One sinner destroys much good.

There is no better exercise
for strengthening the heart
than reaching down
and lifting people up.

Faith

None that trust in God
shall be desolate.

It is hard for those who trust in riches
to enter into the kingdom of God.

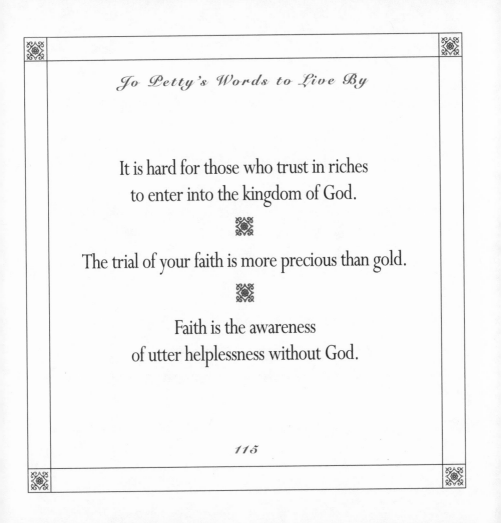

The trial of your faith is more precious than gold.

The trial of your faith is more precious than gold.

Faith is the awareness
of utter helplessness without God.

Faith grows in the valley.

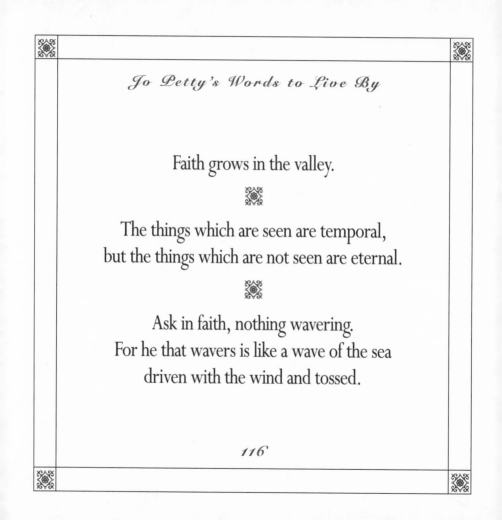

The things which are seen are temporal,
but the things which are not seen are eternal.

Ask in faith, nothing wavering.
For he that wavers is like a wave of the sea
driven with the wind and tossed.

Whatever we beg
of God,
let us also
work for it.

Teach me to live that I may dread
the grave as little as my bed.

Never think that God's delays
are God's denials.

The night is not forever.

A skeptic is one
who won't take
know
for an answer.

Today is the tomorrow
you worried about yesterday.

Prayer is not a substitute for work.
It is a desperate effort to work further and
to be effective beyond the range of one's power.

Don't be afraid to be afraid.

Prayer without work is beggary;
Work without prayer is slavery.

Don't tell me that worry
doesn't do any good.
I know better.
The things I worry about don't happen.

Death is not
extinguishing the light;
it is putting out the lamp
because dawn has come.

Wit's end need not be the end, but the beginning.
The end of man's contriving often is
the beginning of God's arriving.

All I see teaches me to trust
the Creator for all I do not see.

A wish is a desire
without any attempt to attain its end.

Nothing is or can be accidental
with God.

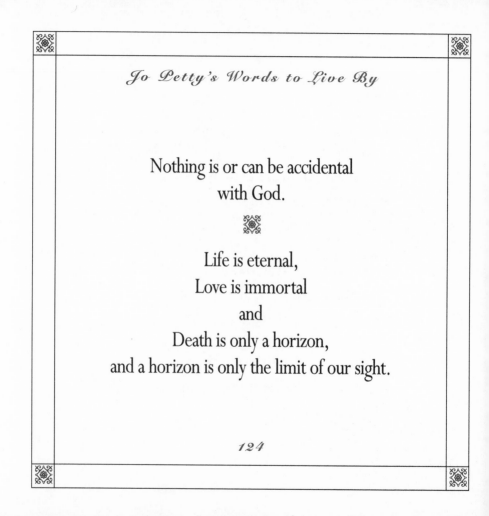

Life is eternal,
Love is immortal
and
Death is only a horizon,
and a horizon is only the limit of our sight.

The only ideas
that will work for you
are the ones
you put to work.

Meekness

The doorstep to the temple of wisdom
is a knowledge of our own ignorance.

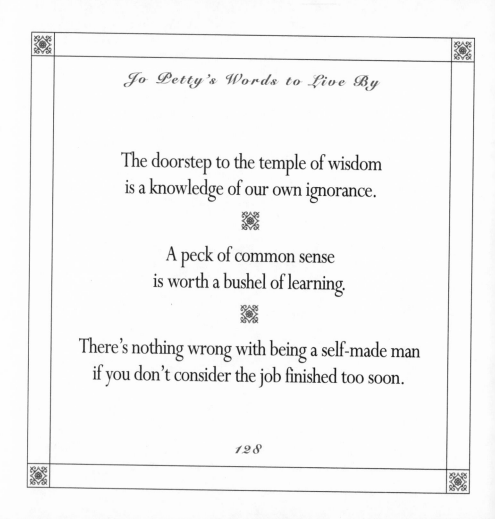

A peck of common sense
is worth a bushel of learning.

There's nothing wrong with being a self-made man
if you don't consider the job finished too soon.

A college education seldom hurts a man
if he's willing to learn a little something
after he graduates.

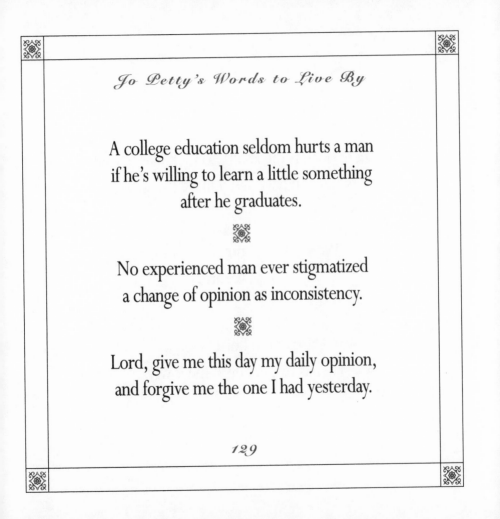

No experienced man ever stigmatized
a change of opinion as inconsistency.

Lord, give me this day my daily opinion,
and forgive me the one I had yesterday.

Nonchalance is the ability to look like an owl
when you have acted like a jackass.

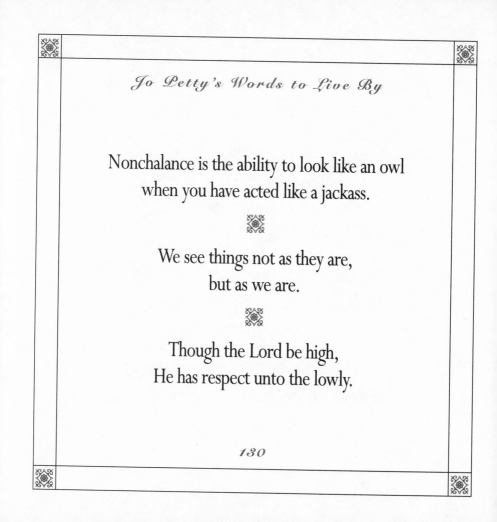

We see things not as they are,
but as we are.

Though the Lord be high,
He has respect unto the lowly.

He tried to be somebody
by trying to be like everybody,
which makes him a nobody.

Every one of us shall give
account of himself to God.
Let us not therefore judge one another.

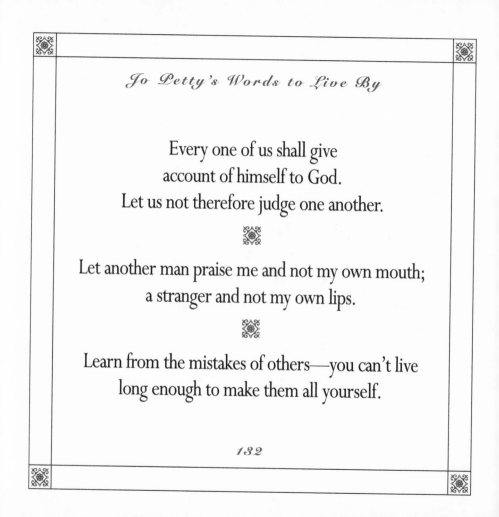

Let another man praise me and not my own mouth;
a stranger and not my own lips.

Learn from the mistakes of others—you can't live
long enough to make them all yourself.

Children should hear
the instruction of their parents.

A meek and quiet spirit
is of great price in the sight of God.

If anyone asks you to go a mile,
go with him two.

A mighty man is not delivered by much strength.

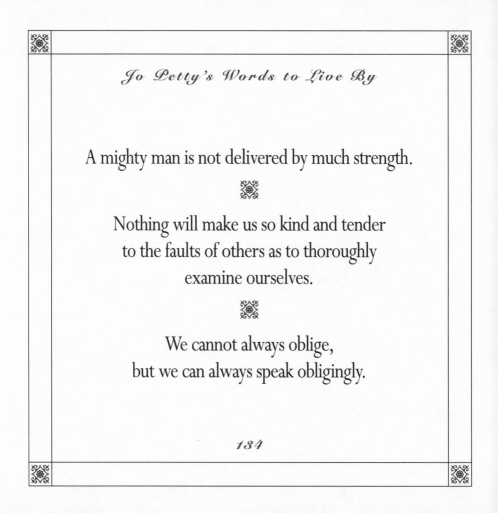

Nothing will make us so kind and tender
to the faults of others as to thoroughly
examine ourselves.

We cannot always oblige,
but we can always speak obligingly.

When success
turns a man's head,
he is facing failure.

Pride makes us esteem ourselves;
vanity desires the esteem of others.

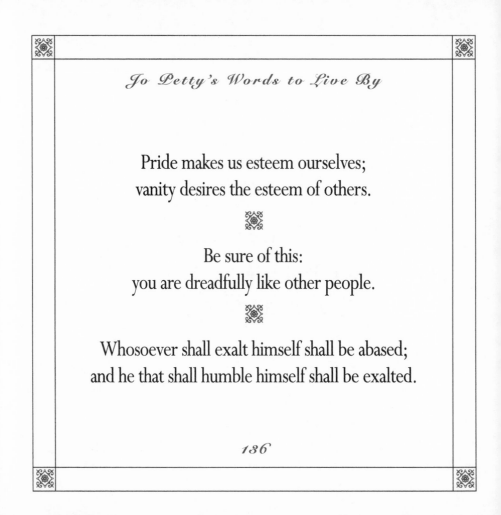

Be sure of this:
you are dreadfully like other people.

Whosoever shall exalt himself shall be abased;
and he that shall humble himself shall be exalted.

There is no surer sign
of perfection
than a willingness
to be corrected.

The wisdom
of this world
is foolishness
with God.

Be not like the cock
who thought the sun rose to hear him crow.

The man who leaves home to set the world on fire
often comes back for more matches.

When you think you stand, take heed lest you fall.

Meekness is not weakness.

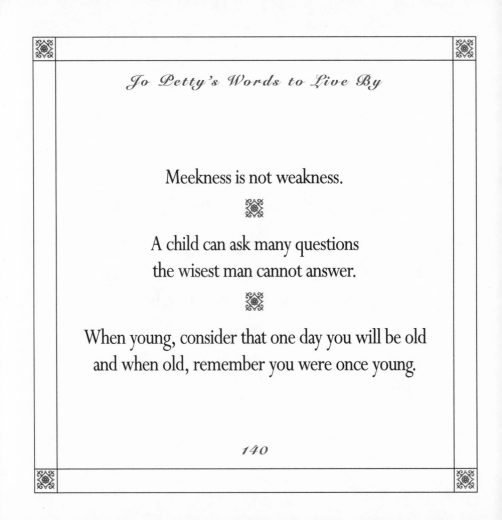

A child can ask many questions
the wisest man cannot answer.

When young, consider that one day you will be old
and when old, remember you were once young.

Teach thy tongue to say, "I do not know."

Temperance

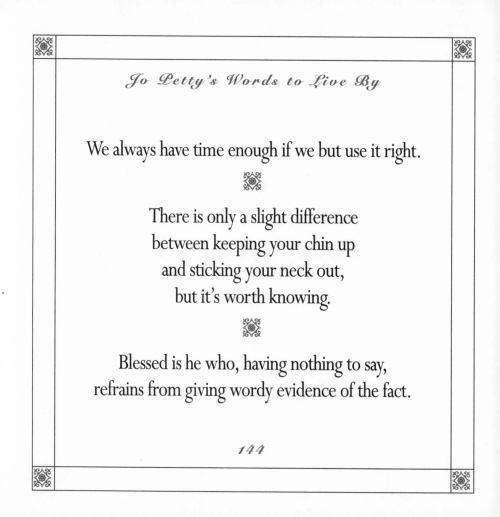

We always have time enough if we but use it right.

There is only a slight difference
between keeping your chin up
and sticking your neck out,
but it's worth knowing.

Blessed is he who, having nothing to say,
refrains from giving wordy evidence of the fact.

Silence is a talent as greatly to be cherished
as that other asset, the gift of speech.

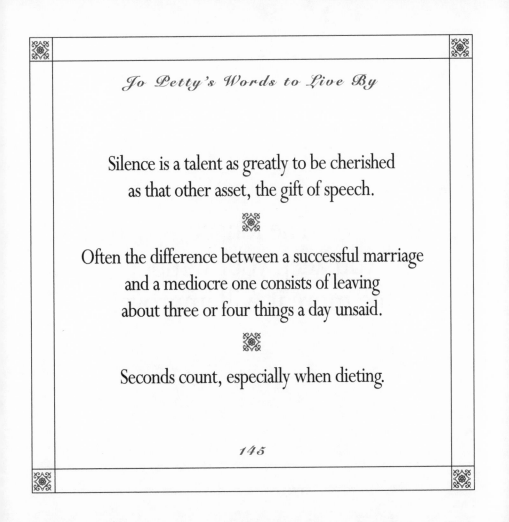

Often the difference between a successful marriage
and a mediocre one consists of leaving
about three or four things a day unsaid.

Seconds count, especially when dieting.

The longer
you keep your temper
the more it will improve.

In any controversy the instant we feel anger
we have already ceased striving for truth,
and have begun striving for ourselves.

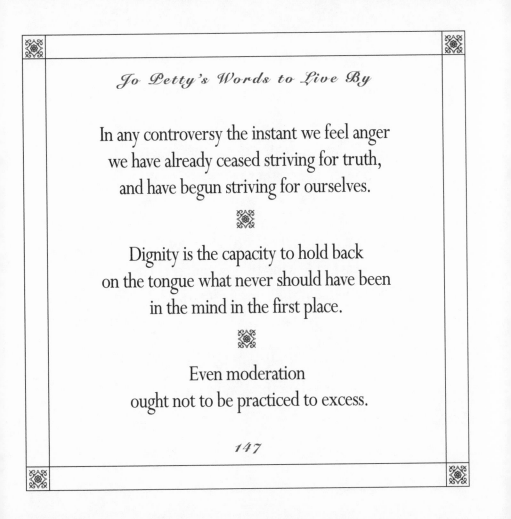

Dignity is the capacity to hold back
on the tongue what never should have been
in the mind in the first place.

Even moderation
ought not to be practiced to excess.

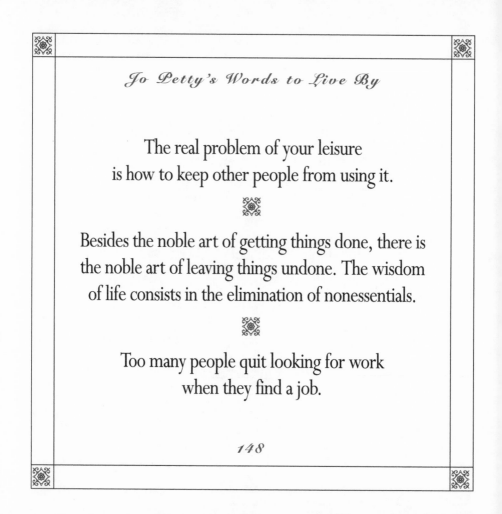

The real problem of your leisure
is how to keep other people from using it.

Besides the noble art of getting things done, there is
the noble art of leaving things undone. The wisdom
of life consists in the elimination of nonessentials.

Too many people quit looking for work
when they find a job.

I have often
regretted my speech,
seldom my silence.

We first make our habits,
and then our habits make us.

The chains of habit are generally too small
to be felt until they are too strong
to be broken.

When a man has not a good reason for doing a thing, he has one good reason for letting it alone.

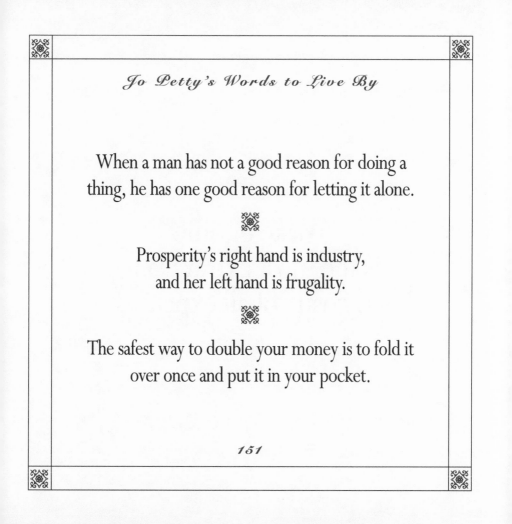

Prosperity's right hand is industry,
and her left hand is frugality.

The safest way to double your money is to fold it
over once and put it in your pocket.

151

Waste of time
is the most extravagant
and costly of all expenses.

A penny saved is as good as a penny earned.

Leisure for men of business
and business for men of leisure
would cure many complaints.

Gold has been the ruin of many.

Wealth is a means to an end
and not the end itself.

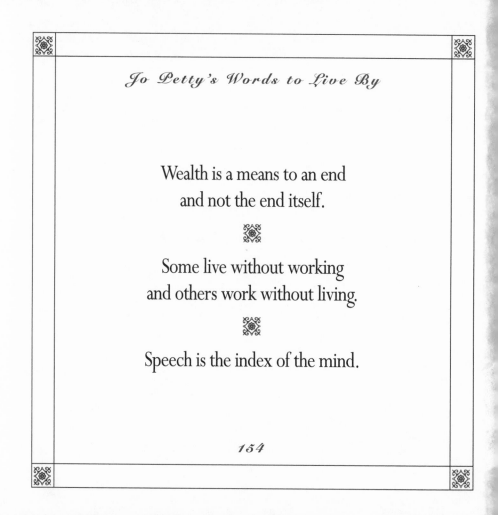

Some live without working
and others work without living.

Speech is the index of the mind.